CARDIFF
THEN & NOW

IN COLOUR

BRIAN LEE & AMANDA HARVEY

The History Press

To James and Alicja Harvey in the year they tie

the knot, 2012.

First published in 2012

The History Press
The Mill, Brimscombe Port
Stroud, Gloucestershire, GL5 2QG
www.thehistorypress.co.uk

British Library Cataloguing in Publication Data.
A catalogue record for this book is available from the British Library.

ISBN 978 0 7524 7113 6

Typesetting and origination by The History Press
Production managed by Jellyfish Print Solutions
Printed in India

CONTENTS

ACKNOWLEDGEMENTS

We would like to thank all those people who, over the years, have loaned us their photographs for inclusion in *Cardiff Then & Now* and the other books which we have compiled for The History Press. These books include *Cardiff Remembered*, the two Cathays, Maindy Mynachdy and Gabalfa books, the two Central Cardiff books, *Cardiff Voices*, *Cardiff's Vanished Docklands*, *Yesterday's Cardiff*, *The Welsh Grand National - from Deerstalker to Supreme Glory*, *Butetown and Cardiff Docks* and, more recently, *A Postcard from Cardiff*. Special thanks for their help go to Tony Woolway chief librarian at Media Wales and Katrina Coopey and her staff at the Central Library local studies department. Thanks are also due to all those authors, living and dead, whose books we have quoted from. And finally to Jessica Andrews at The History Press and all those involved in the production of this book. We apologise if we have inadvertently omitted anyone from these acknowledgements.

ABOUT THE AUTHORS

Author and freelance writer Brian Lee has lived in Cardiff all his life. He has published twenty-one books on the history of Cardiff as well as numerous magazine and newspaper articles.

Freelance motoring journalist Amanda Harvey is Cardiff born and bred. In this, her second title, she joins forces with her father, local historian Brian Lee. Amanda is currently the assistant editor at *Morris Minor Magazine*, formerly *Minor Monthly*, the best-selling international magazine for Morris Minor enthusiasts worldwide.

INTRODUCTION

Cardiff, the capital city of Wales, is a city of change. Residents of the town even back in the 1860s were commenting sadly on the rapid changes that were taking place. What those long-gone Cardiffians would think of their town today (Cardiff became a city in 1905) if they could somehow once again walk the same streets, one can only guess.

Even in my photographer daughter Amanda Harvey's short time here the city has seen many transformations. This book reveals these changes, mainly in the heart of the city. The ancient Golate and Womanby Street, perhaps the oldest two streets in the city, are featured, along with the city's most famous landmarks, Cardiff Castle and the City Hall.

The Queen Street area of Cardiff was well known for its abundance of theatres and cinemas – such as the Capitol, Empire and Queen's. These picture palaces no longer exist but the reader will now be able to see where they actually stood and what business or shop has replaced them. In some cases, like the old library in Trinity Street, the buildings have hardly altered in a hundred years. However, it is interesting to see the changes that have taken place around them by comparing the old photographs to the new.

Younger Cardiffians will now be able to identify the places that their parents or grandparents once told them about, while their parents and grandparents will look back with nostalgia at the places of their past, like the old Capitol Ballroom and Café in Queen Street when during the big band era of the 1950s, they went to see Joe Loss, Stan Kenton, Eric Winstone, The Squadronaires, Harry Gold, Ted Heath's Orchestra, accompanied by singers Dickie Valentine, Denis Lotis and Rita Rosa, and many other big bands at those popular Sunday evening concerts.

Also vanished are department stores such as Roberts on Kingsway and David Morgan Ltd on The Hayes, which are now just memories.

CARDIFF CASTLE

IN 1883, LORD Bute gave orders that carved animal figures should be mounted on the walls of the castle. There were long and detailed discussions as to the size and choice of the animals, and it wasn't until some five years later that Lord Bute's instructions were finally completed. The first models included a seahorse and a pelican.

THE ANIMALS WERE moved to their present site, nearer to Cardiff Bridge, in 1928, when figures of a vulture, a beaver, a leopard, racoons and an anteater were added along with a bear, which replaced the original polar bear. However, Rita Spur, writing in *The Lady* in 1959, claimed that the vulture, beaver, leopard, anteater and racoons were not added until 1931 and that they were the work of Alexander Carrick RSA, of Edinburgh. Some Cardiffians have

complained that the tourist shop and ticket office seen to the left of the new photograph spoils the view of Cardiff's most famous landmark.

THE CLOCK TOWER

CARDIFF CLOCK TOWER can be seen in the photograph opposite in around 1903, when the 'animal wall' still stood in front of Cardiff Castle. Generations of Cardiffians and visitors to the city have been telling the time by this magnificent clock. The tower was built between 1869 and 1873 and was designed by William Burgess. It contains a complete suite of apartments, which include a winter smoking room, a summer smoking room and a bachelor's bedroom.

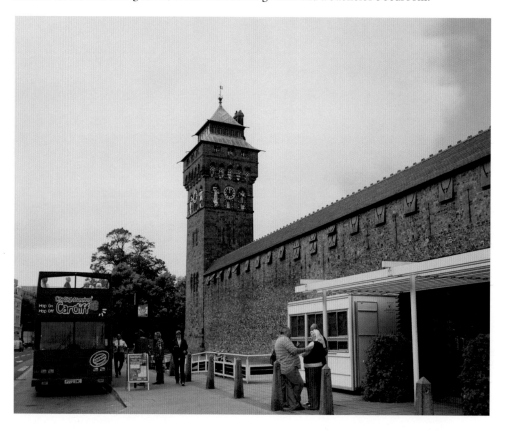

THIS FOUR-SIDED Victorian clock, which was built in Liverpool, stopped at 12 p.m. in 2011. Many people think that the plant growing on the castle walls is ivy, but it is actually grape vines! The timbered battlement box on the castle wall, as seen in the old photograph, has been removed, and horse-drawn trams were still in evidence when this postcard picture was taken at the beginning of the twentieth century. In contrast, in the modern photograph above the official city sightseeing 'hop on, hop off' bus, which takes tourists on a tour of the city, can be seen.

DUKE STREET AND
CASTLE STREET

DUKE STREET, C.1920 (left). Cardiff Tramways purchased a prototype double-decked, covered-top tram in 1923 which seated sixty-four people. A further eighty trams of similar style were purchased over the next two years. Between 1536 and 1810, this road was known as Shoemaker Street. It was widened in 1924 when the row of shops abutting on the castle wall was demolished. Originally called Duckstrete, the name suggests an association with poulterer's shops. However, some romantics say it owes its name to the sojourn of the Duke of Normandy in Cardiff Castle for more than twenty-five years.

THE TRAMS SEEN in the distance in the old photograph are travelling along Castle Street, which at one time had houses on both sides of the street (along with a row of shops which backed on to the castle walls). However, as these dwellings caused something of a bottleneck to the city's increasing traffic they were removed. The white building in the centre of the new photograph is the Angel Hotel, and local legend has it that an underground passage connects the castle with the hotel. During the summer months, the lawn in front of the castle wall is populated with picnickers.

WOMANBY STREET

WOMANBY STREET, C.1890 (opposite). This was the scene of a battle between pirates in 1759, when a fight took place between the crew of a ship named *The Eagle of Bristol* and the crew of a man-o-war called *Aldrough*. The crews were armed to the teeth and at the end of the battle, one man lay dead and many were injured. Womanby Street was known as Hundemanby (from around 1270) and the name is thought to mean 'the home or dwelling of the hound man or keeper of hounds'.

IT WAS ALSO known as Red Cow Lane at one time because there was a pub of that name in the street. The Red Cow stood next door to the Horse and Groom pub, located where the white van can be seen in the new photograph. The red brick building on the left was once the site of Trinity Chapel, the first Nonconformist church in Cardiff.

CITY HALL

CITY HALL, C.1906. At a meeting of the County Borough of Cardiff on 6 December 1897, it was resolved: 'to empower the Corporation to erect and maintain in the said park (Cathays) a Town Hall.' On that day competitive designs went on display in the assembly room of the old

Town Hall, and a few days later Mr Alfred Waterhouse RA, acting as a competition assessor to the fifty-six architects whose designs had been put forward, awarded the first prize of £500 to Lanchester, Stewart and Rickards of London.

SIX YEARS LATER, during the first half of 1900, work was commenced when a dwarf wall and railings were constructed around the one-acre site. Cardiff was granted city status in 1905; a year later, Lord Bute declared this magnificent Portland stone building open. The old photograph shows a circle of lawn in front of the building. In the new photograph, two young ladies can be seen sitting in front of the fountain (which was built many years after the lawn was created).

15

THE LAW COURTS

THE CIVIC CENTRE complex, including the Law Courts, City Hall and the Welsh National Museum, in the early 1960s. A man and woman can be seen passing the statue of Judge Gwilym Watkins, stipendiary judge and squire. The Law Courts, the work of architects Lancaster, Stewart and Rickards, are in the English and French Renaissance style and were

skilfully designed to be in harmony with the City Hall. Two wonderfully designed cupolas surmount the eastern façade, and – like the City Hall – the building was completed in 1906.

WITH THE NATIONAL War Memorial in Alexandra Gardens, the National Museum of Wales, the University College and the County Hall buildings – to name just a few – there are few cities in the world that can boast such a fine architectural wealth of sculpture in so small a space.

17

THE GLAMORGANSHIRE CANAL

THE GLAMORGANSHIRE CANAL was opened in 1794 as a means of transporting iron from Merthyr Tydfil to Cardiff Docks. The last barge passed down it in 1942. The old photograph on the left was taken in around 1906. The Glamorganshire Canal was one of the picturesque features of old Cardiff: 25 miles long, with some fifty-two locks. The canal flourished for more than a century. The £103,600 cost of its construction was met by traders and Merthyr's ironmasters. From North Road, the canal followed the path of the old town wall and moat. On the east side of Cardiff Castle, the canal travelled under Kingsway through what is now a pedestrian subway. From there, it passed along The Friary to what was appropriately called The Tunnel.

SADLY, ALL THAT remains of the canal in the Cardiff area is some 1,500 yards at the Forest Farm Nature Reserve in Whitchurch. A car park now runs along North Road where once the canal used to flow.

THE RED LION,
KINGSWAY

THE RED LION Hotel, Kingsway, can be seen on the right of the old photograph on the left. It stood on the east corner of what was then Smith Street and North Street. At the beginning of the nineteenth century, when there were no Catholic churches in Cardiff, Mass was once said in the ordinary room of this inn.

THE RED LION was still serving pints as recently as 1958. The underground ladies' and gentlemen's lavatories to the left of the older photograph survived the demolition of the pub – which was pulled down to make way for Evan Robert's store – for a short while. The horse and cart seen in the photograph is passing another well-known watering hole, the Rose and Crown, which had stood on the site since 1787. It was demolished in 1974, and a new Rose and Crown pub was built near the site; this was renamed Coopers in 1997, and later became The Barfly.

21

THE POUND

KINGSWAY, C.1950. The gentlemen's lavatory was built on the site of the town pound. The pound had a hole in one of its walls through which farmers could see if any of their horses or cows had strayed and been impounded. The same spot, many years earlier, had been the site of the north gate of the town wall, and all traffic to or from the north had to pass under a castellated tower.

THE TOWN WALL, which was some 10 feet high and 6-8 feet thick, had been constructed in the fourteenth century: the longest surviving section of it, near The Hayes, finally vanished in 1901,

when it was pulled down to make way for the old Fish Market (a site to be later occupied by the South Wales Electricity Board's showroom) and now vacant, after being briefly occupied by Habitat.

THE NEW THEATRE

THE NEW THEATRE, built by Messrs Runtz & Ford, was opened on the 10 December 1906. The productions staged were varied and included music hall, drama, opera, variety and pantomime. You name it, the 'New' has staged it! Cardiff's first music hall was probably the Coliseum, which stood in Bute Street, where, it was said, 'melodrama and farce (plus a pint of beer) could be had for threepence'. Cardiff's first purpose-built theatre was the Theatre Royal, constructed in 1826

THE NEW THEATRE, CARDIFF.

on part of the ground where the Parc Hotel in Queen Street now stands. Other early theatres were the wooden Circus Theatre (1876) in Westgate Street; the 'new' Theatre Royal (1878) in St Mary Street; and the Grand Theatre (1887) in Westgate Street, later to be known as the King's and then the Hippodrome.

MANY FAMOUS PEOPLE have trod the New Theatre's boards: Anna Pavlova, Max Miller, Tommy Handley, Gracie Fields, Marlene Dietrich, Bette Davies, Laurel & Hardy, Tom Jones, Shirley Bassey – the list goes on and on. To the left of the new photograph one can see the Park Plaza Hotel, which opened in 2005 and is a 4-star, deluxe, 129 bedroomed, state-of-the-art hotel. It was awarded 'AA Hotel of the Year' in 2007-08.

WOOD STREET

THE 'NEW' THEATRE Royal, on St Mary Street and Wood Street, can be seen on the right of the old photograph, *c.*1910. It opened in 1878 and had two imposing façades, the one Gothic and the other – which was added in 1900 – in a Classical style. Many of the leading acts of the day trod its boards, but sadly it was completely gutted by a fire in 1899. When it was rebuilt it was renamed the Playhouse (1920), and then the Prince of Wales in 1935.

TODAY, IT IS A Wetherspoon's pub, but remnants of the old theatre can still be seen inside this historic building, which has a preservation order. The tram in

the older photograph is seen passing Tom Langdon's tobacconists, which was on the corner of Wood Street and St Mary Street. Langdon's was known to Cardiffians as 'the bear shop' because of the stuffed Russian bear that used to stand by the door. That same bear can now be seen in the tobacconist shop in Wyndham Arcade. Wood Street was named after Colonel Wood, who owned land in the area.

THE CAPITOL CINEMA

THE CAPITOL CINEMA, which opened in 1921, had a restaurant and dance hall. It not only provided its patrons with a cinema but also a restaurant, dance hall and music from an orchestra. Many famous film stars paid a visit to the cinema to promote their films, including

Charlton Heston, Ray Milland, Danny Kaye, Gene Autry, Roy Rogers and Ronald Regan – later, of course, to become President of the United States.

THE CAPITOL CLOSED on 21 January 1978. It was demolished in 1982, as were the block of small shops alongside it, to make way for the Capitol Exchange Centre, which began business in 1990. The new photograph is taken from the middle of the road in Windsor Place, directly opposite to where the Capitol once stood.

WORKING STREET

ST DAVID'S HALL had not been built when the picture of Working Street below was taken in the 1960s. Many Cardiffians will remember the old and established ironmonger's Cross Brothers,

which was situated in this street. This photograph was taken near what was then the Central Library; in the distance, on the extreme left of the picture, can be seen Mackross' store, which closed some years ago.

THE CENTRAL LIBRARY is now The Cardiff Story Museum. Working Street, which is now a busy thoroughfare running from St John's Street to The Hayes, appears on Speed's map of 1610. As can be seen, it has changed dramatically since the older photograph was taken. The 2,000-seat St David's Hall, the national concert hall of Wales, was officially opened by Queen Elizabeth, the Queen Mother, on 15 February 1983, though the first concert had taken place there in 1982.

THE PARK HALL CINEMA

THE PARK HALL Cinema, *c.*1962. The cinema was opened as a concert hall in 1885, and on 2 July 1892 a 'Grand Reception Concert' was held at the Park Hall for the Rt Hon. Lord Mayor of London, Alderman David Evans, and his wife, the Lady Mayoress. The artistés included the

Welsh Ladies Choir, comprised of 150 voices. Also on the bill was 'A Band of Harps', under the leadership of Miss Annie T. Jones; the conductors of the choir were Mrs Clara Novello Davies and Mr Jacob Davies. Balcony seats cost 3s and front seats 2s. Park Hall became a cinema in 1916, and a certain Mr Winston Churchill once lectured there.

THE LAST FILMS to be shown at this magnificent picture house were *Operation Crossbow* and *Seven Brides for Seven Brothers*. It was sadly demolished in 1980. Bellini's Restaurant is now situated over the old cinema's entrance. The Park Hall was just one of a number of theatres and cinemas that were situated in the town centre. The King's Theatre in Westgate Street and the Prince of Wales in St Mary Street are just two others that have disappeared.

THE QUEEN'S CINEMA

THE QUEEN'S CINEMA was known as the Picture Show in 1910 and was later called the Cardiff Cinema Theatre. In 1929, it had the distinction of being the first cinema in Cardiff to show 'talkies'. They presented *The Singing Fool*, which starred Al Jolson, then 'the world's greatest entertainer'.

THE QUEEN'S CINEMA was well known in the 1950s for showing the old black and white horror films such as *Frankenstein*, *The Werewolf* and *Dracula*. However, the last film to be screened there (on 29 October 1955) was *The African Queen*, which starred Humphrey Bogart and Katharine Hepburn. Demolished in 1960 to make way for John Menzies and Littlewoods, the site is now occupied by Game and Specsavers. Like the pubs the Alexandra Hotel, Park Vaults, Taff Vale, Tivoli and the Red Lion, many of the popular stores that used to be in Queen Street, including Seccombes, Mackross, Marments, Masters, Littlewoods, Millets, Woolworth and C&A, have disappeared. In 1985, the British Home Stores, which had opened on the site of the old Carlton Hotel in 1955, moved to bigger premises on the opposite side of the street, on the site of the former Woolworth store.

THE EMPIRE THEATRE

THE EMPIRE THEATRE in Queen Street, 1925, can be seen opposite. The Empire began life as Levino's Hall in 1887. It became the Empire Theatre in 1889 and many famous acts trod its boards. During the Second World War, one Cardiffian recalled the Empire in a local newspaper:

Who, of the elderly residents of Cardiff, will ever forget the old Empire Music Hall?
It was the most popular entertainment house in the country. What comradeship it
inspired amongst the big audiences! What enthusiasm! All the stars came to the Empire:
Sir Harry Lauder, George Robey, Charles Coburn, Dan Leno, Marie Lloyd, Little
Tich, Vesta Tilley, Harry Tate, Albert Chevalier, Zena Dare – and many others.

HE COULD HAVE added the great Harry Houdini to that list. The theatre had a unique feature: a sliding roof, which was opened during the interval to give theatre-goers some fresh air. The Empire was later known as the Gaumont Cinema and closed in 1960. C&A stood on its site when the store came to Cardiff in 1963, but closed forty years later, in 2003; Primark is now situated on the site.

CROCKHERBTOWN

A DIRECTORY FOR 1858 informed its readers that on the approach to the villas in Crockherbtown there were to be found neatly-kept flower beds, while dwarf shrubs and evergreens greeted the increasing number of respectable inhabitants. The Cardiff to London stagecoach used to pass through Crockherbtown, and the first letter box was erected there in 1855. In 1866, the Town Council changed the name 'Crockherbtown' to Queen Street. The old photograph on the left shows Spital Cottages, Crockherbtown, in 1883.

TO THE LEFT of the modern photograph can be seen a block of luxury apartments; this building was once the AA building, Fanum House. The Taff Vale Railway Office, with its well-known clock tower (built in 1860), was situated on this site but was demolished in 1973. The shops in the picture are part of the Capitol Exchange Centre, which celebrated its twenty-first birthday in 2011.

TRANSPORT

A LOCAL PAPER dated 1 May 1902 informed its readers that: 'At noon today the Cardiff Corporation Electric Tramways were successfully opened for traffic, amidst the general rejoicing of everyone concerned, and Cardiff can claim to be one of the progressive towns

of the kingdom which have adopted electricity for traction purposes.' Earlier that day, twelve tramcars, decorated with imitation flowers and flags bearing the Welsh dragon, left the Clare Road depot for the Town Hall where the mayor, council officials and invited guests were waiting to be taken on a trip around the town. Some £380,000 had already been spent upon the new tramways and when completed the total cost would be around £500,000. However, in 1931 motor buses replaced trams on the Cathays route, and by 1939 the Corporation had decided to replace trams with trolley buses. When this Queen Street picture was taken in around 1949, the days of the prototype double-deck covered tram were nearly at an end.

ON 20 FEBRUARY 1950, the last Cardiff tram made its final journey. Pedestrians can now walk along Queen Street without having to worry about being knocked down.

PARADISE PLACE

OF THESE FIVE businesses in Queen Street, only the Midland Bank – to the extreme right of the picture, and now known as HSBC – remains today. The Taff Vale pub stood on the corner of Queen Street and Paradise Place, which no longer exists. The Taff Vale pub was demolished in 1978 after standing on the same site for nearly a century. The windows to the left of the

old photograph are actually in Paradise Place, described in the *Cardiff Borough Records* as: 'A narrow street off the south side of Crockherbtown, parallel with the west side of Charles Street.'

SAM ALLEN, IN his *Cardiff Reminiscences*, gives us a much better description of the Paradise Place of the 1860s: 'The name Paradise Place sounds highly poetical, and no-one today would associate that locality with the Garden of Eden, yet some of us can remember very picturesque little suburban cottages, with pretty front gardens, and quite a natty little blacksmith's shop.' Some older Cardiffiians will remember the Cardiff Comrades' Club, which stood on the same side as the Taff Vale pub – where local legend has it that singer Shirley Bassey once sang. Paradise Place led to Ebenezer Street, where once stood the Ebenezer Church, which was built at a cost of £850 and opened on 3 December 1829. It was demolished in 1974, along with other buildings in the area. Incidentally, Oscar-winning Hollywood film star Ray Milland once stayed in the Taff Vale Inn before he became famous; he lived for a short time in Cardiff.

CHARLES STREET

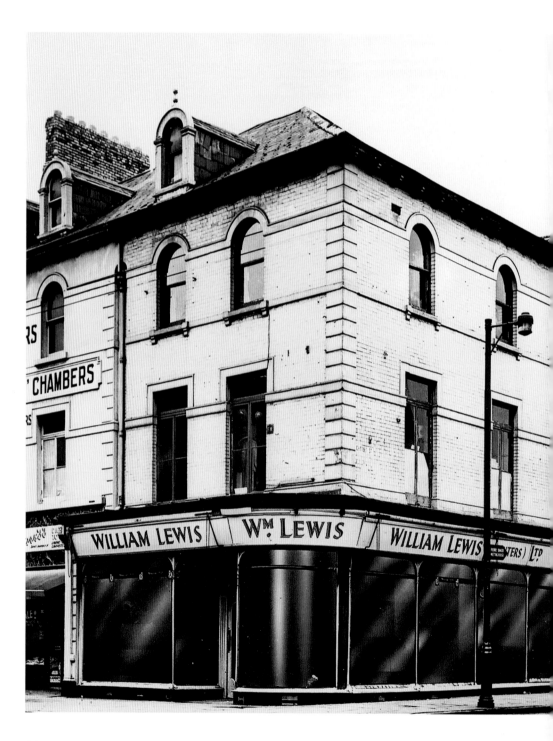

CHARLES STREET HOUSES St David's Roman Catholic Cathedral, which was bombed during the last war. The street is named after Charles Vachell, who was elected mayor on two occasions (1849 and 1855). He played a big part in the implementation of the Public Health Act (1848) in Cardiff, because of his concern over the living conditions of some of the inhabitants of the town. The first mention of Charles Street appears in Piggot's Directory of 1835. William Lewis, the stationer's, occupied the corner of Queen Street and Charles Street when the old photograph on the left was taken in 1965.

LEWIS'S IS NOW a Burger King restaurant. Business offices and restaurants have taken the place of the houses that were once occupied by the town's elite. Marks & Spencer have been situated on the opposite corner of Charles Street for many years, and it is hard to believe that there was a time when huntsmen and their pack of hounds would meet at this spot to go foxhunting.

QUEEN STREET

QUEEN STREET, C.1904. William Rees, author of *Cardiff: A History of the City* writes: 'In 1855, Queen Street within the walls was said scarcely to deserve the name of a street for it was merely a lane with about twenty-four houses linking St John Street to Crockherbtown, the presence of the weighing machine obstructing the street and its approach.' This certainly wasn't the case when this postcard picture was taken. Rees continues: 'Cardiff indeed, during the latter half of the 19th century, was acquiring the trappings of a modern borough, its

communications greatly improved. As early as 1855, horse buses were running every half-an-hour from the Queen's Hotel to the railway station and the dock, marking a new stage in the growth of public transport.'

QUEEN STREET HAS seen many changes over the years and stores such as Mackross, Marments (1879-86), Swears & Wells, Wilsons, Woolworth and 2007 boutique which stood adjacent to the now vanished Andrews Arcade, and which some older Cardiffians will remember, have all disappeared. Once one of the main shopping areas in central Cardiff, the street is now little more than a gateway to the lively St David's shopping centre.

WESTGATE STREET

THE HEADQUARTERS OF the fire brigade stood in Westgate Street from 1917 until 1973. It was not the first in the town: when the New Town Hall was built in St Mary Street in 1850, a fire engine house was constructed nearby (in 1853), at the rear of the New Town Hall running into Westgate Street. The station was of Victorian design, and when it was condemned it took some considerable time and effort to demolish due to the early use of reinforced concrete. The River Taff once flowed through Westgate Street, but in 1849 work began on diverting the course of the river, thus reducing the threat of flooding in the central area of the town.

IN 1973, THE station moved again, this time to Adam Street under the South Glamorgan Fire and Rescue Service. The old Westgate Street site is now a multi-storey car park. The area created by diverting the river became Cardiff Arms Park, now the site of the Millennium Stadium.

JONES COURT

JONES COURT, SITUATED off Womanby Street, has been preserved to some extent. The terraced houses in Jones Court were built in the 1830s by the Marquis of Bute to house his workers during the construction of Cardiff Docks.

THERE ARE TWO more recent plaques on the wall of the entrance to the courtyard. The first states that it was erected by the 1915 Cardiff Corporation Members of the Property and Markets Committee, with the Lord Mayor, Alderman J.T. Richards JP, and Councillor A.C. Kirk JP, the chairman. The other plaque was unveiled on the 19 February 1982 to commemorate the official opening of Jones Court by the Rt Hon. the

Lord Mayor of Cardiff, Councillor Ronald F. Watkiss, CBE. The terraced properties now house a number of businesses.

ST JOHN'S CHURCH

OLIVERS' SHOE SHOP, on the corner of Church Street and High Street, can be seen in the photograph below. In the centre of both images the church of St John the Baptist can be seen.

This has stood in the centre of Cardiff for over 800 years. This medieval building was severely damaged during the revolt of Owain Glyndwr at the beginning of the fifteenth century and was replaced, in 1443, by one built in the Perpendicular style. The tower was added in 1473 and now contains a fine peal of ten bells, which are rung regularly for Sunday services and on civic and national occasions.

OLIVERS' OCCUPIED THIS building (left) for many years, but in 1997 it became a showroom for kitchens. The Co-operative Bank and Greggs replaced the shops at the corners of Church Street. As with many churches today, St John's requires constant care and attention and is therefore fortunate to have an organisation named 'The Friends' who work to help to preserve this place of worship for the future – much to the benefit of Cardiffians and visitors. A group of volunteers serve light refreshments from Tuesday to Saturday in the vestry.

THE SYNAGOGUE

THE SYNAGOGUE WAS originally a church. This picture was taken in 1957 and initially known as the Cardiff New Synagogue, and later still as the United Synagogue. To the right of the picture is Austin Reed, the gentlemen's outfitters.

AUSTIN REED'S BUILDING has now been taken over by Barclays Bank. The synagogue has also gone: it closed on Shabbos, on the first day of January 1954, when the lease ran out. Unfortunately, the building was knocked down to make way for an office block which, in its turn, was transformed into a restaurant in 1998. An illustrated notice board in Wetherspoons' Central Bar informs us that the name of the Wetherspoon pub recalls the Central Congregational Chapel, built before the synagogue on the site. It was one of around sixty Nonconformist places of worship in Cardiff, along with the English Presbyterian Church, also in Windsor Place.

ST JAMES' CHURCH

THE CHURCH ON the left of the old photograph is the Roath Road Wesleyan Methodist Church, which was opened in 1871 and was almost demolished when it was bombed during the Second World War. St James' church, on the right, was consecrated on 15 June 1894 and was closed quite recently. This card is from around 1905. This Grade II listed church was built as a 'chapel' of St John, the city centre church. The church of St James the Great was erected to serve the parochial area of Tredegarville and the Newport Road area in 1894. Lord Tredegar, Godfrey Charles Morgan, donated the site to the parish. St James the Great suffered serious fire damage in 1925. It is

thought that the fire broke out somewhere in the vicinity of the choir vestry, and the altar and stained glass windows were all badly damaged.

ST JAMES' CELEBRATED its final act of worship on 16 September 2006. Just in front of the tower of St James' stands the Cardiff Royal Infirmary Chapel, built after the First World War. Where the Roath Road Wesleyan Methodist church once stood now stands Eastgate House, also known as Heron House, which was completed in 1969.

HIGH STREET

A VISITOR TO the little town of Cardiff 160 years or so ago would have found the debtor's prison, Town Hall and Butter Market all situated in High Street and handily placed near the old quay. In 1829, the fact that High Street was considered the best business street in Cardiff so annoyed the tradesmen of Duke Street that they issued a broadsheet proclaiming their wares.

The photograph on the left shows the High Street in Cardiff in 1928. The entrance to Cardiff Castle can be seen in the centre, and there is a Rolls-Royce parked on the extreme right.

THE STATUE OF the 2nd Marquess of Bute, erected in High Street in 1853 and later moved to the centre of the roundabout at the bottom end of St Mary Street, can now be seen in Bute Square. The Griffin Inn, whose sign can be seen (advertising Pale Ale) to the left of the old photograph, is now long gone. The High Street's road and pavements had recently been refurbished when the new photograph was taken.

QUAY STREET

QUAY STREET IS situated on the corner
of St Mary Street and High Street
and leads to Westgate Street, where
the River Taff once ran. It bears little
resemblance to the Quay Street of
old, which was frequented by sailors,
fishermen and farmers leading their
cattle to the slaughterhouse at the end
of the street.

IN THE 1960s, Anthonie, the gown
shop – as can be seen in the old
photograph – stood on the one corner,
and the Trustee Savings Bank, now a
Costa café bar, on the other. Anthonie
was just one of the many shops sold by
Messrs Stephenson and Alexander,

the old established chartered auctioneers and estate agents who still operate from the High Street. The new office building above Jacobs' is now Loosemores Solicitors.

THE
TOWN
HALL

THE OLD TOWN Hall in St Mary
Street, *c.*1900. This building
replaced the Guildhall in High
Street. Cardiff's first Town
Hall, which was also known
as the Town House, Bothall or
Guildhall, was erected half-way
along High Street in 1331. A
replacement Guildhall – which
featured a Georgian façade
and a double flight of stone
steps flanked by an ironwork
balustrade – was opened in
1747. With the increase in the

population in the days when 'coal was king' and the subsequent opening of the Bute Docks, it soon became clear that a much larger Town Hall was needed. An acre of land between St Mary Street and Westgate Street was put aside, and building commenced in 1849. (During the work earlier walls were found, and a circular stairway of great depth, thought to be part of the old town's defences, was also uncovered.)

OPENED IN 1853, the New Town Hall also housed the old post office, police court and parade ground, as well as the fire brigade offices and rates office. The Julian Hodge's Commercial Bank of Wales, or Hodge House, is now situated on the site of the old Victorian Town Hall, and houses a number of call centres and offices.

JAMES HOWELLS

ST MARY STREET, *c.*1904. (The sign to the right of the handcart points to the Bethany Baptist chapel which used to be in Wharton Street.) On 21 October 1865, James Howell opened his warehouse in Stuart Hall on The Hayes; it was so successful that he quickly moved to larger premises in St Mary Street, on the site of the present building (seen on the right of both photographs). Expansion of the building soon followed, and by 1883 he had acquired Biggs Brewery to the rear of the store, which afforded a small frontage on Trinity Street. By 1892,

the store comprised almost
36,800 square feet, making
it one of the biggest retail
establishments in Wales. A new
grocery department proved
popular, and was followed –
in 1913 – by the opening of
a motors showroom on the
opposite side of Bakers Row.

IN 1931, A new four-storey
building was opened on the
corner of Wharton Street and
St Mary Street to house a new
menswear department. Many
improvements to the store
followed over the coming years
and, in 1972, the department
store business was divided from
the motors division and was sold
to House of Fraser. The taxi rank
seen in the new photograph is a
recent innovation.

THE GOLATE

THE OFFICES OF the *Western Mail* and *South Wales News* on St Mary Street opposite Wharton Street, *c*.1930. The *South Wales News* later became the *South Wales Echo*. The building was called Golate House, and Golate Lane is to the right. In the days when newspapers were produced by the old hot-metal method, the building was the fourth home of the *Western Mail* and from 1930 this paper – along with its sister paper, the *South Wales Echo* – were produced in the building until 1960.

THE GOLATE, WHICH can be seen on the extreme right of the new photograph, leads from St Mary Street to Westgate Street. One of Cardiff's best-remembered thoroughfares, this ancient lane once contained four dwelling houses, five stables and a blacksmith yard – all said to be let for a yearly rental of *2s 6d*! It has variously been known as Porth Llongau, Ships Gate, Frog Lane, Golygate and Gulleygate. One long-gone Cardiffian recalled that 'during heavy rainfalls The Golate was one tumultous and surging stream of dirty waters racing down to the river, which then lay where Westgate Street now stands.' Hinchly's, which can be seen in the modern photograph above, have now moved to Newport Road.

ST MARY STREET

ST MARY STREET in 1909. 'Once upon a time St Mary Street was made up of town houses of the local gentry. Lewis of the Van, Mathews of Llandaff, Basset of Beau Pre, each had their town residence to which they would come during the winter months,' according to *Cardiff: Notes Picturesque and Biographical* by J. Kyrle Fletcher. St Mary Street derives its name from the old parish church of St Mary, which is thought to have dated from the eleventh century and which was washed away in the great flood of 1607.

IN 1910, AN old Cardiffian recalling the
St Mary Street of his youth had this to say:

*St Mary Street was known as 'The Parish'. The
river came right round the west side of the street
and flowed over the spot now occupied by the
Royal Hotel. The street at this portion, in windy
weather, was a dangerous place to pass because
of the tremendous gusts which swept across
the moors. I have seen the tide washing over the
footpath of St Mary Street and I recollect one
fine day seeing a man run across St Mary Street
from his house and taking a header into the
river. Mr John Batchelor had a builder's yard,
where he built small vessels, just this side of
where the Great Western Hotel now stands and
which, of course, abutted onto the river.*

St Mary Street was a highway long before
the city of Cardiff was built. The now
pedestrianised St Mary Street had a makeover
in 2011, and many of the bus routes which
used to go through this ancient street were
diverted into Westgate Street.

DAVID MORGAN LTD

DAVID MORGAN'S, IN The Hayes, in 1904. David Morgan commenced trading in 1879, at
No. 23 The Hayes. The following year he took over the adjoining building on the south corner of

Barry Lane. By 1884, he had become so successful that he had extended his business southwards along The Hayes and a five-storey building was erected. Later, the acquisition of land between the rear of the Royal Arcade and Tabernacle Lane enabled him to increase the depth of the store. When George Hopkins's grocery store became available, he acquired this too and built a second five-storey shop. The St Mary Street store was opened in 1898, and the following year the Morgan Arcade was completed.

CARDIFF'S MUCH LOVED family-run department store, David Morgan Ltd, closed its doors in January 2005, having provided thousands of South Walians with an unrivalled service for 125 years. In September 2007, Borders Bookshop took over part of the building but sadly closed down in December 2009. The building is now home to fifty-six one- and two-bedroom apartments. The David Morgan clock has been a familiar landmark for generations of Cardiffians. It was made by Gillet & Johnson of Croydon and erected in 1904. However, by 1986 it had become rusted beyond repair and an exact replica in fibreglass was made by Gillet & Johnson from the original drawings (which they still had filed away).

THE FREE
LIBRARY

THE FREE LIBRARY in The Hayes in the early years of the
twentieth century (right). The central library in Trinity
Street owed its beginnings to Mr Peter Price, a local
architect who made several attempts to implement the
adoption of the Public Libraries Acts, 1850-1855. When
the acts were implemented in 1862, the entire contents
of a voluntary library in St Mary Street were handed over
to the Corporation. Cardiff was the first local authority
in Wales to adopt the Acts and provide a public library.
This building in The Hayes was opened in 1882 and
forms the northern end; the southern end was completed
in 1896 and was opened by the Prince of Wales, later
King Edward VII. John Ballinger was appointed librarian
in 1884. He resigned as chief librarian in 1908 when he
took the post of chief librarian at the National Library
of Wales at Aberystwyth. For more than 100 years the
old library served Cardiffians well, and many people will
have fond memories of it.

THE FREE LIBRARY, now partly obscured by trees, is currently The Cardiff Story local history museum and tourist centre. One can see by looking at the old photograph how these trees have grown over the years. The John Batchelor 'Friend of Freedom' statue was erected in 1886, and although it has stayed in The Hayes ever since, it has been moved a few yards on several occasions. When it was erected a petition was signed by 1,200 people who demanded its removal. A staunch Liberal and a public-spirited man, this controversial figure had many enemies. John Batchelor was a Radical Liberal and his obituary in the *Western Mail* claimed: 'In all municipal and Parliamentary contests he was in the forefront of the battle, but he made political enemies, which no doubt helped to account for the failure of his once prosperous ship-building business, and his financial difficulties.'

THE SOUTH WALES
ELECTRICITY BOARD
SHOWROOMS

HILL STREET, *c.*1950 (left). Many Cardiffians will recognise the building shown here as the South Wales Electricity Board Showrooms, which stood on the corner of The Hayes and Hill Street. When the building was first opened, on Shrove Tuesday, 19 February 1901, by Councillor Thomas Andrews, it was advertised as 'The New Wholesale Fish, Poultry, Bird, Game, Fruit and Vegetable Market.' It was built on the site of the old St John's Infant School and the eastern side of the building joined the Glamorganshire Canal. The cars seen in the old photograph are parked in Canal Street, and to the right can be seen the railings of the bridge over the canal.

IN JUNE 1937, the building was converted to the City Electricity Committee Show Rooms and Offices. The building was later occupied by Habitat, but ceased trading in 2011.

PARK HOTEL

PARK HALL BUILDINGS, Queen Street. The Park Hotel, on the right, was built in the French renaissance style in 1885. Built on the edge of parkland, where the magnificent civic centre now stands, the concert hall, which was part of the Park Hotel, and now known as The Parc, has been a popular Cardiff landmark since it was first opened in 1885. The first major modernisation was in 1935 – the hotel was still rooted in the Victorian age, and had brass bedsteads and net curtains.

This revamp brought wall-to-wall carpeting, built-in wardrobes and easy chairs, with a writing table, in each of the 115 rooms.

MAJOR REFURBISHMENTS WERE made in 1996 when it became the forty-ninth hotel to carry the brand name of Thistle, one of the UK's leading hotel groups. In 2006, a massive fire devastated the building, and fifty fire fighters battled the flames as 100 guests were evacuated. However, two years later The Parc proudly revealed its new look.

THE MECURE
HOLLAND HOUSE HOTEL

THE JULIAN HODGE Building, Newport Road, can be seen in the photograph opposite *c*.1967. There are still some residential houses left in Newport Road, but most of them have made way for offices and stores such as The Range, Argos, Homebase, Marks & Spencer and Halfords to name but a few.

THE MECURE HOLLAND House Hotel today replaces the Julian Hodge Building in Newport Road. The building also housed businesses Chartered Trust plc and ACL Life. Mecure Holland House Hotel is a four star hotel and is classed as one of Cardiff's luxury hotels. The hotel opened in the spring of 2004. The hotel's 165 bedrooms offer guests a range of accommodation options including executive rooms and spacious suites, some of which offer particularly inspiring views over the city and contain panoramic windows so guests can enjoy and absorb every detail of Cardiff's suburbs.

THE ROYAL HOTEL

THE ROYAL HOTEL, St Mary Street, can be seen in the photograph below *c.*1890. The Royal Hotel was built at the costly sum of £15,000 by the Cardiff Hotel Co. It opened its doors in April 1866 and was described by the *Cardiff Times* as 'a really first-class hotel worthy of the metropolis of Wales'. The Royal Hotel has survived a number of fires, changes and takeovers

over the years. The biggest change perhaps was in 1896, when the extension of the hotel took the building to the corner of Wood Street. The then owner explained, in a local newspaper, that it had been 'largely extended, refurbished and decorated'. Many famous people have rested their heads at this historic hotel, from Elizabeth Taylor and Richard Burton to Lord Haw Haw – and, of course, Captain Scott and his crew dined at the Royal Hotel on 13 June 1910 before setting off on the *Terra Nova* on their ill-fated Antarctic expedition.

TO THE RIGHT of the new photograph can be seen the historic Pierhead Clock mechanism, which was unveiled to signal the end of the improvement to the work on St Mary Street and High Street in the autumn of 2011. The 100 year-old mechanism was originally installed at the Pierhead Building in Cardiff Docks, now Cardiff Bay, in 1897.

DUKE STREET ARCADE

DUKE STREET ARCADE, *c.*1910 (opposite). The arcade leads into High Street and St John's Square, and was built around 1902. High Corner House in the street was demolished in 1877.

DUKE STREET ARCADE, which was designed by architects T. Waring and J.P. Jones, leads into High Street Arcade, which was built in 1885. The arcades opened for the first time on a Sunday in 1996. In 1924, the row of shops abutting the castle wall was knocked down to make the street wider. Sam Allen, in his *Cardiff Reminiscences*, writes: 'in mid-nineteenth-century Duke Street, formerly called Shoemaker Street, the shops and houses were of a whimsical architecture.' A Grade II listed building, Duke Street Arcade is one of Cardiff's shorter arcades. Several Cardiff arcades have disappeared over the years, the most recent being Andrews Arcade in Queen Street, which was demolished when improvements were made to the area a few years ago. Others that have vanished from the scene are Queen Street Arcade (1866-1987) and the short lived Oxford Arcade on The Hayes (1970-2006). Dickens Arcade, which used to be in Castle Street, is another arcade that has vanished in living memory.

MORGAN ARCADE

MORGAN ARCADE, C.1910. Morgan Arcade, perhaps the best preserved of Cardiff's Victorian arcades, is named after David Morgan, who started out in business with a gentlemen's outfitters on The Hayes. The building of this arcade is said to have altered the whole aspect of this part of the city, as it swept away a nest of slums, plus some picturesque courts and gardens. At the St Mary Street end it wiped out a large house with a large garden belonging to a well-known

Victorian figure in Cardiff, Mr Charles. At
The Hayes, it cleared away the Union
Buildings, consisting of thirty-three houses
and small shops and an inn. It was built in
1879, the architect being Edwin Seward and
the developer David Morgan.

OPENED IN 1896, Morgan Arcade has
entrances on The Hayes and St Mary Street.
With its first-floor Venetian-style windows
and original slender wooden shop fronts, it
has a number of shops worth a visit including
Spillers Records, the oldest record shop in
the world. Established in 1894, the shop
relocated from The Hayes to Morgan Arcade
quite recently. In total, Cardiff can boast an
array of Edwardian and Victorian arcades
which stretch to some 2,655 feet. Since
medieval times, local people were granted
plots of land known as *burgages* or *heys*, *heys*
meaning specifically an area of land enclosed
by a hedge. The name The Hayes is therefore
probably derived from that ancient word.

HIGH STREET ARCADE

COURTS' FURNISHING STORE on High Street, *c*.1970. High Street Arcade, which was built between 1880 and 1887, was designed so that one could walk from High Street directly to St John's Street (or St John's Square, as it is popularly known). It was originally 50 yards long and had thirty-four shops with offices above. Of High Street, we learn from William Rees's *Cardiff: A History of the City* that: 'Within the walled town, the main north-south artery was the High Street, with its continuation in St Mary Street, stretching in unbroken line from the gate of the Castle to the South Gate of the town. The High Corner marked the junction of High Street with Duke Street and Shoemaker Street.'

LIKE THE OTHER arcades of Cardiff, High Street Arcade has seen many shop changes over the years. What would the Cardiffians of yesteryear think of Looby Loo's Boutique, Lunacy Boutique, Pussy Galore and Uncaged Beauty? One of its oldest shops must surely be the Joke Shop.

CITY OF ARCADES

HIGH STREET ARCADE was opened between 1880 and 1887. It was designed to make it possible for shoppers to walk from High Street directly to St John's Square. Cardiff was in fact once known as 'the city of arcades'.

THE HIGH STREET Arcade was a great success from the beginning. Just like the other arcades in the town, it has contributed to the success of Cardiff as a shopping centre. A well-known resident of Cardiff recalled that when he was a boy and living in the Valleys, his mother returned from a visit to Cardiff and told him of 'the splendid new street with a glass roof'. High Street Arcade, like most of the other Cardiff arcades, is well-designed architecturally, and although the shops and businesses have changed many times over the years it still retains its old-world atmosphere.

ROYAL ARCADE

THE ROYAL ARCADE, *c.*1879. Cardiff's oldest arcade is the Royal Arcade, built on a Burgage plot of land known as Tabernacle or Collier's Court. It was designed by Peter Price and reported to have been built by Philip Burgess, a Somerset man who arrived in Cardiff in 1854. Some local historians suggest that it was built in 1855. However, as Jennie Savage points out in *Depending on Time*, 'this cannot be possible, as the Cardiff Arcade Co., that created and financed the arcade, was not formed until 1868'.

THE *SOUTH WALES Echo* reported in 2005 that the Royal and Morgan arcades were to get a revamp, which traders will hope boost business as part of a £10 million investment in the area.

UNIVERSITY COLLEGE OF SOUTH WALES AND MONMOUTHSHIRE

UNIVERSITY COLLEGE, CARDIFF.

THE UNIVERSITY COLLEGE of South Wales and Monmouthshire opened at Newport Road in the old Cardiff Infirmary building, otherwise known as Glamorgan and Monmouthshire Infirmary. It first opened its doors in 1883, and the new institute was formally established by Royal Charter the following year. The old photograph on the left shows the college sometime in the early years of the century.

SOME CARDIFFIANS MAY recall the University being demolished in 1960 to make way for the University of Engineering building, seen here.

WOOD STREET
CONGREGATIONAL
CHURCH

WOOD STREET IN the early 1970s. The Wood Street Congregational church can be seen to the right. The church was the first building to be built in Wood Street in 1864 as a Temperance Hall.

It was later converted into a music hall and circus. One of the largest buildings in the country at the time, it could seat 3,000 people. The last service to be held there was in November 1971 and two years later, in 1973, it was demolished.

RECALLING THE OLD music hall, Sam Allen in his *Cardiff Reminiscences* wrote: 'For a long time both circus shows and melodramatic performances took place alternatively. A short play generally of a blood-curdling character followed by a circus turn, or acrobatic performance on the flying trapeze or suspended from the ceiling.' Wood Street – named after Colonel Wood, who owned the land – linked the area called Temperance Town with St Mary Street. And like many other parts of central Cardiff, the area has seen many changes over the years. There are plans to demolish the tacky central bus station terminus, which lies off Wood Street and which as stood there since 1954, and build a modern one.

Other titles published by The History Press

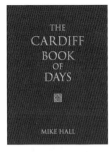

The Cardiff Book of Days

MIKE HALL

This book contains a quirky or important event or fact about Cardiff for every day of the year. Featuring all manner of events from different periods of history, many of these are historically significant, such as Cardiff's elevation to city status, or quirky, entertaining and amusing, like Billy the Seal's escape from the lake in Victoria Park. There are sombre commemorations of German air-raids that killed many of the city's residents, and great sporting triumphs by Wales, Cardiff City and Glamorgan.

978 0 7524 6008 6

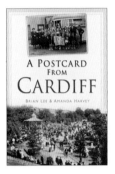

A Postcard from Cardiff

BRIAN LEE & AMANDA HARVEY

Drawing on their detailed knowledge of the city's history, in this book Brian Lee and his daughter Amanda Harvey take the reader on a pictorial journey of the Cardiff of yesteryear. A fascinating selection of archive postcards has been chosen to reflect the changing fashions and pastimes in the city. They also show changes in types of transport, and the developing character of streets and districts as they took on the form that is familiar today. This book is sure to enthral anyone who knows and loves this vibrant city.

978 0 7524 5836 6

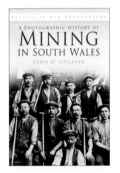

A Photographic History of Mining in South Wales

JOHN O'SULLIVAN

The South Wales Valleys once boasted the richest coalfields and the best anthracite coal in the world. Before the dawn of the twenty-first century all but one of the hundreds of coal pits were closed, destroying jobs and whole communities. Only Tower Colliery at Hirwaun continued to produce coal, thanks to the bid by the miners to keep working. This book salutes those to who Wales – and the world – owes so much.

978 0 7524 5941 7

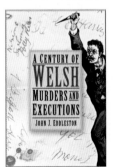

A Century of Welsh Murders and Executions

JOHN J. EDDLESTON

Thirty-six murderous tales that shocked not only Wales but also made national headlines. This fascinating new book covers every twentieth-century murder committed in Wales which resulted in a judicial execution. They include the case of William Augustus Lacey, who killed his young wife with a razor in a fit of jealously at Pontypridd in 1900, and baby farmer Rhoda Willis, the first woman to be hanged at Cardiff Prison. This enthralling text will appeal to anyone interested in the shady side of Welsh history.

978 0 7509 4961 3

Visit our website and discover thousands of other History Press books.

www.thehistorypress.co.uk